W9-CQO-672

Deschutes Public
Library

UNDERSTANDING
------- OUR -------
ORGANS

LUCY BEEVOR

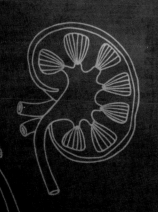

capstone

© 2017 Heinemann-Raintree
an imprint of Capstone Global Library, LLC
Chicago, Illinois

To contact Capstone Global Library please call 800-747-4992, or visit our web site www.capstonepub.com
All rights reserved. No part of this publication may be reproduced or transmitted in any form or by any
means, electronic or mechanical, including photocopying, recording, taping, or any information storage
and retrieval system, without permission in writing from the publisher.

Edited by Brenda Haugen
Designed by Russell Griesmer and Jennifer Bergstrom
Original illustrations © Capstone Global Library Limited 2016
Picture research by Jo Miller
Production by Jennifer Bergstrom
Originated by Capstone Global Library Limited

20 19 18 17 16
10 9 8 7 6 5 4 3 2 1

Library of Congress Cataloging-in-Publication Data
Names: Beevor, Lucy, author.
Title: Understanding our organs / by Lucy Beevor.
Description: North Mankato, Minnesota : Capstone Press, [2017] | Series:
 Raintree perspectives. Brains, body, bones! | Audience: Ages 8-11. |
 Audience: Grades 4 to 6. | Includes bibliographical references and index.
Identifiers: LCCN 2016036102|
ISBN 9781410985798 (library binding) |
ISBN 9781410985835 (paperback) |
ISBN 9781410985958 (eBook PDF)
Subjects: LCSH: Organs (Anatomy)—Juvenile literature. | Human
 biology—Juvenile literature. | Human anatomy—Juvenile literature.
Classification: LCC QM27 .B44 2017 | DDC 611—dc23
LC record available at https://lccn.loc.gov/2016036102

Acknowledgements
We would like to thank the following for permission to reproduce photographs: Dreamstime: Varandah,
7; Newscom: Science Photo Library/Steve Gschmeissner, 20, ZUMA Press/Bryan Smith, 21; Shutterstock:
Angallen Rogozha, 13, Blend Images, 27, Cessna152, 6, Christos Georghiou, 22, CLIPAREA l Custom
media, 11, deja15, 29, design36, 9, dr OX, 17, Hurst Photo, 19, joshya, 23, Luciano Mortula, 5, Monkey
Business Images, 18, Picsfive, 25, sciencepics, cover, 14, Sebastian Kaulitzki, 24, Tefi, 15; design elements:
Shutterstock: designelements, PILart, Ohn Mar, Nadydy, Studio_G

Every effort has been made to contact copyright holders of material reproduced in this book. Any omissions
will be rectified in subsequent printings if notice is given to the publisher.

All the internet addresses (URLs) given in this book were valid at the time of going to press. However, due
to the dynamic nature of the internet, some addresses may have changed, or sites may have changed or
ceased to exist since publication. While the author and publisher regret any inconvenience this may cause
readers, no responsibility for any such changes can be accepted by either the author or the publisher.

Printed and bound in the USA
010049S17CG

TABLE OF CONTENTS

HUMAN ORGANS

Lots of people work together to make life in a city possible. Some people work in bakeries and restaurants, making food. Police and firefighters make sure the city is safe. And other people keep the city clean. Everyone has a job to do.

Your body is kind of like a city too. Every organ in the human body has an important job to do. Your lungs help you to breathe. Your heart pumps blood through your body. And your brain controls everything. In your body, your organs work together to keep you alive.

Everyone in a city has a job to do, just like every organ in your body works to keep you alive and healthy.

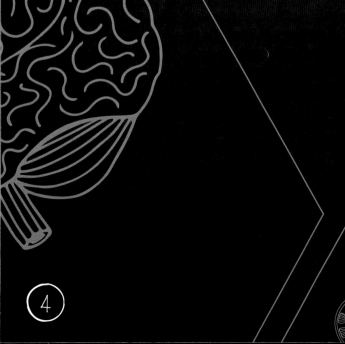

Organs are grouped together into organ systems. For example, your stomach, small intestine, and large intestine make up your ***digestive system***. These organs break down the food you eat for energy. This process is known as digestion. The organs in each system work together to do a particular job.

ORGAN POWER

Can you name your body's largest organ? Is it your brain? No. Maybe your heart or lungs? Nope! The body's largest organ isn't inside the body at all. You see it and touch it every day. It's skin! In fact, the average adult has between 6 and 8 pounds (2.7 and 3.6 kilograms) of skin.

Your skin covers and protects the rest of your body. It keeps your *internal* organs on the inside, where they belong. But your skin does more than just hold you together. Skin keeps dirt and germs out of your body. It also stores water, fat, and vitamin D for the body to use.

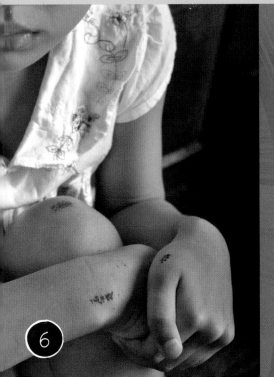

Body Talk

Did you know that skin heals itself? When you fall and scrape your knee, *cells* in your skin work to form a blood clot over the wound. This then turns into a scab, which is a bit like the body's own protective bandage. Eventually the scab falls off, revealing a fresh layer of healthy skin below.

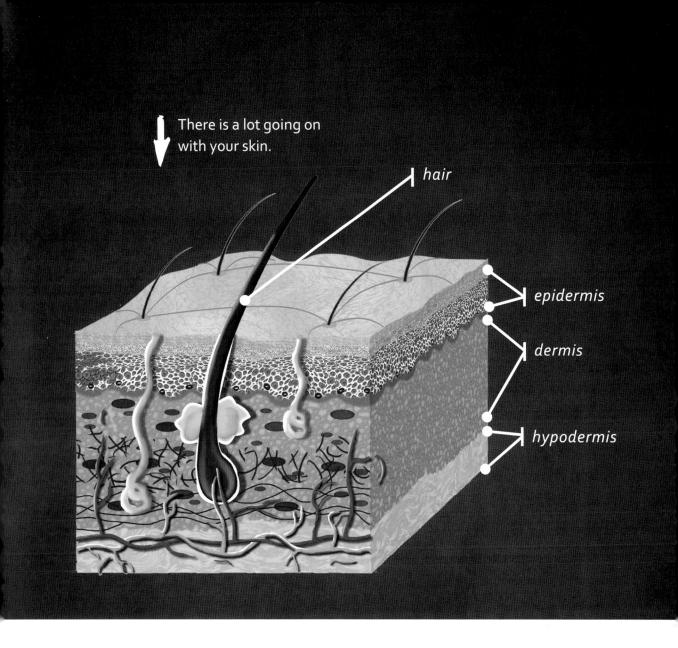

There is a lot going on with your skin.

hair

epidermis

dermis

hypodermis

Living Layers

Skin is made of three layers. The outer layer is the epidermis. It provides a barrier to the outside world. It is thickest on the parts of your body that see the most wear and tear, such as your feet. The middle layer of skin is the dermis. It contains sweat glands, blood vessels, and hair follicles. It also has nerve endings that sense touch and temperature. The hypodermis is the deepest layer. It attaches the skin to underlying bone and muscles.

Under the Skin

If you could peel away your skin, you would find muscles underneath. Muscles are organs too. The heart is both a muscle and a major organ, while some muscles help other organs to do their jobs. The bladder is a muscle-lined pouch that stores urine until you go to the bathroom. Without the muscles surrounding your bladder, you would not be able to control the need to go to the bathroom.

If you stripped away all your muscles, you would find your bones. Like muscles, bones are also organs. All of these bones make up the skeleton. Your skeleton supports your body and allows you to stand up and walk. Some of the large bones also have an important job. They make blood cells in their soft, spongy centers. The spongy center of a bone is called bone marrow.

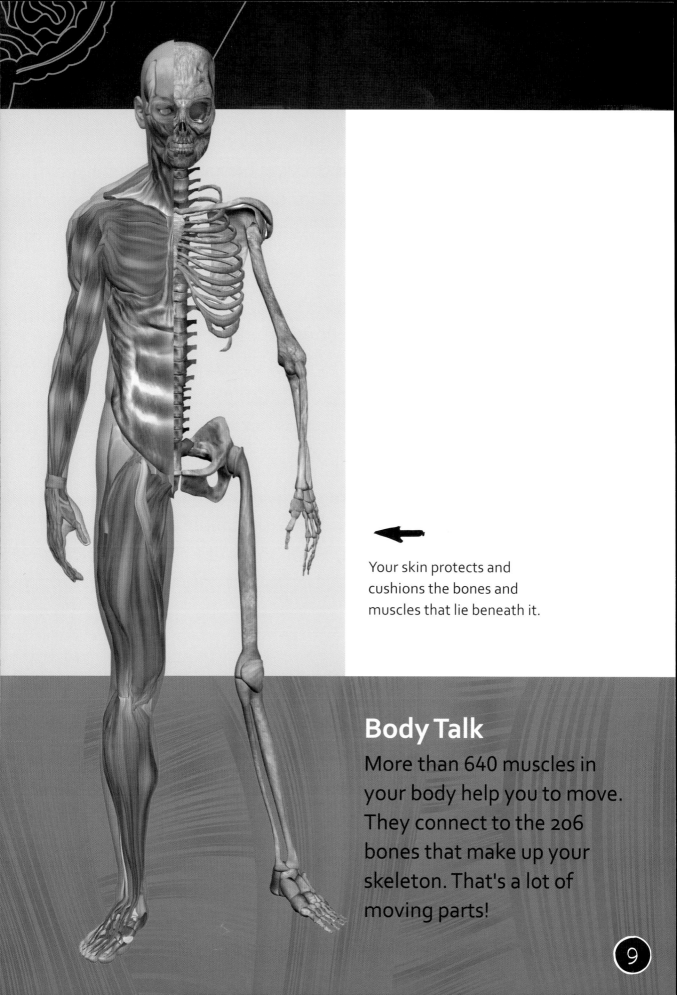

Your skin protects and cushions the bones and muscles that lie beneath it.

Body Talk

More than 640 muscles in your body help you to move. They connect to the 206 bones that make up your skeleton. That's a lot of moving parts!

VITAL ORGANS

When most people think of organs, they picture the ones in the chest and **abdomen**. Lying beneath your ribs, the lungs and heart are major organs you couldn't live without.

Take a Deep Breath

Your lungs are two squishy, pinkish organs that look like sponges. Breathe in. Can you feel your chest getting bigger? Your lungs have filled up like a balloon. When you breathe in, **oxygen** is brought into your lungs. Your body needs oxygen to survive.

You also use your lungs to talk. When you breathe out, air passes over your **vocal cords**. Air rushing over closed vocal cords makes sounds. Without lungs, you wouldn't be able to talk, sing, laugh, or live!

See for Yourself

Place a hand on your chest. Now take a deep breath in, and hold it for a few seconds. Does your hand rise? That's because your lungs inflate, like a balloon, when you breathe in. Release the breath, and your hand falls again. Your lungs have pushed the air back out, deflating like a balloon without air.

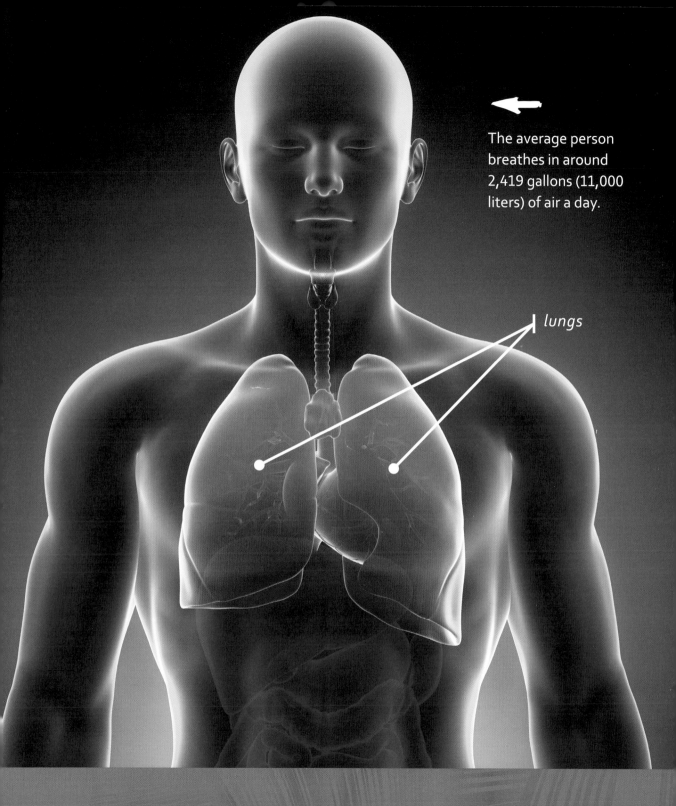

The average person breathes in around 2,419 gallons (11,000 liters) of air a day.

lungs

Body Talk

Sometimes your **respiratory system** gets a little mixed up, and you get the hiccups. The "hic" sound is caused by your vocal cords slamming shut.

Feel the Beat

Your heart is safely nestled between your lungs. This important organ is about the size of your closed fist. But it doesn't look much like a Valentine's Day heart. Your heart actually looks more like a pear.

Blood picks up oxygen as it flows through your lungs. Then it travels to the heart. When the left side of the heart is filled with blood, the heart squeezes tight like a fist. This squeeze squirts your blood though tiny tubes called blood vessels. The blood vessels carry blood and oxygen to the rest of your body.

All the cells in your body use oxygen from your blood. They replace the oxygen with **carbon dioxide**. Blood carrying carbon dioxide goes to the right side of your heart. From there, this blood is pumped to your lungs. Carbon dioxide leaves your body every time you breathe out.

Body Talk

Every time your heart squeezes, it causes your heart to beat. Your heart beats about 300 million times a year.

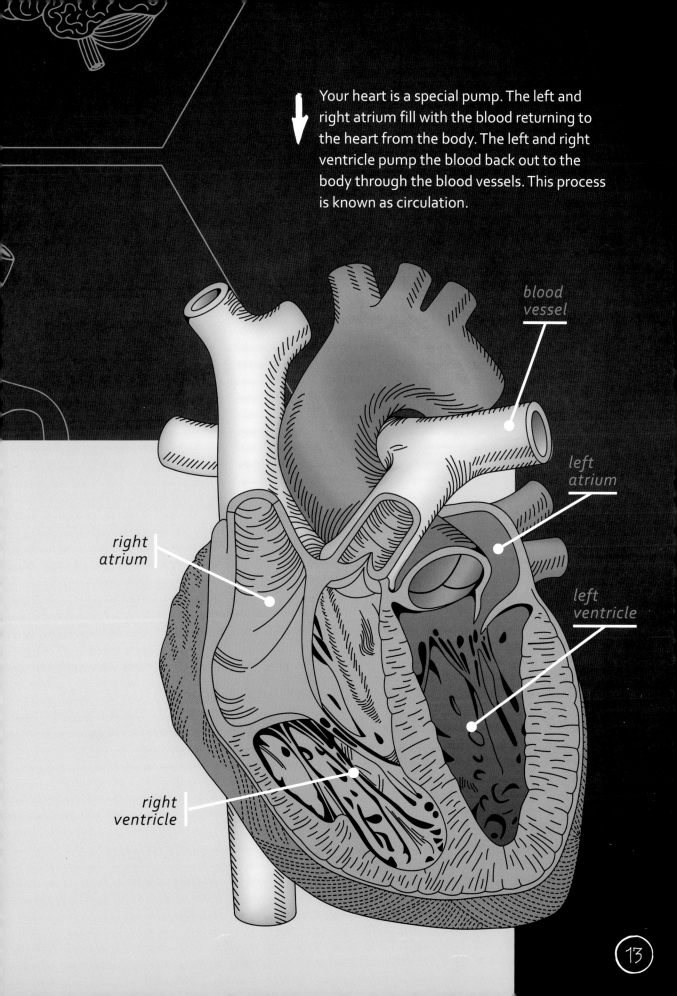

Your heart is a special pump. The left and right atrium fill with the blood returning to the heart from the body. The left and right ventricle pump the blood back out to the body through the blood vessels. This process is known as circulation.

blood
vessel

left
atrium

right
atrium

left
ventricle

right
ventricle

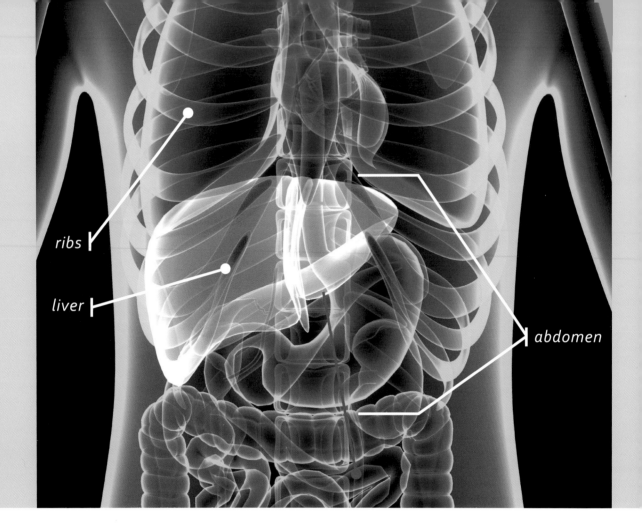

ribs

liver

abdomen

↑ The liver is known as the body's laboratory because it performs around 500 jobs.

The Liver Delivers

Like your heart and your lungs, the liver is an organ you couldn't live without. In fact, the liver is your largest internal organ. In adults, this wedge-shaped, spongy organ is about the size of a football.

The liver has many important jobs. Your liver makes a liquid called **bile** that breaks down the fat you eat. It also stores vitamins and energy that your body needs. But the liver's most important job is cleaning your blood.

The Green Organ

Behind the liver is a small, pear-shaped organ called the gallbladder. Unlike most of your organs, this one isn't dark red. It's actually green! The color comes from the bile that the gallbladder stores. When you eat a large meal, your body needs more bile than your liver can supply all at once. The gallbladder stores extra bile to help digest the extra food. Although the gallbladder is an important organ, the body can survive without it.

At around 3 inches (8 centimeters) long, the gallbladder is a tiny organ. However, it is part of the largest system in the body, the digestive system.

liver

gallbladder

Body Talk

If your liver stopped working, you would die in about 24 hours. But you don't need your whole liver. Even if 75 percent of your liver were removed, you would be able to survive.

The Spleen

On your left side below your liver, you have a soft, purplish-red organ called the spleen. This fist-shaped organ is about the same size as your heart. The spleen *filters* your blood to get rid of germs. You can live without your spleen. But people who have had their spleens removed are ill more often.

The Growler

Like the spleen, the stomach lies just below the liver. Your stomach is the organ that growls when you are hungry. This stretchy, muscle-lined sack holds the food you eat. The stomach mixes food with digestive juices. These chemicals begin breaking down food to release energy for the body.

These major organs make up the digestive system. In an average human lifetime, the digestive system handles up to 55 tons of food and liquid!

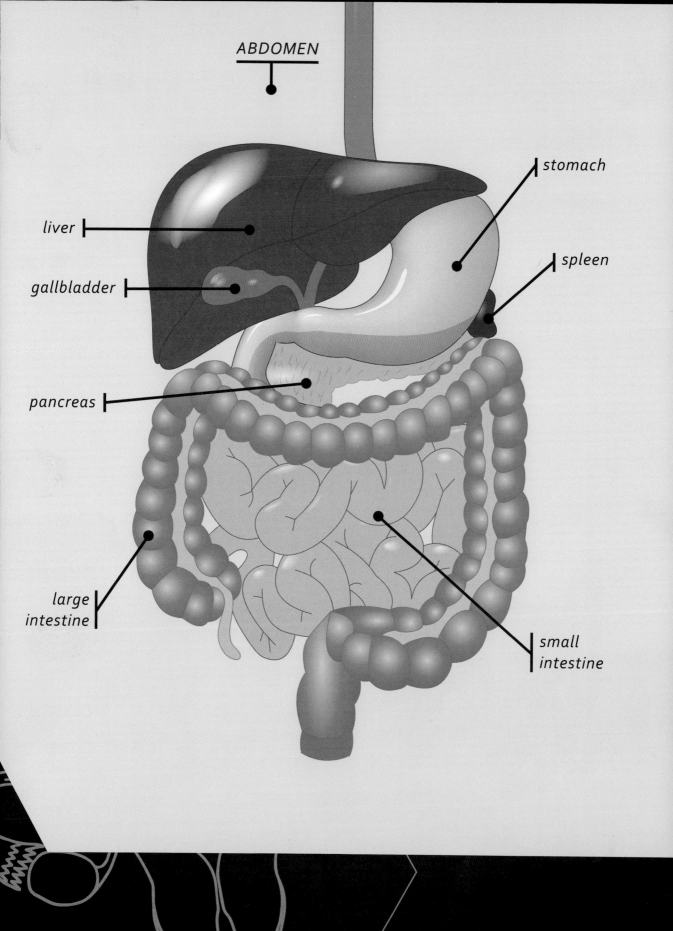

ABDOMEN

stomach

liver

spleen

gallbladder

pancreas

large
intestine

small
intestine

17

MOVERS AND SHAKERS

Below your stomach lies an army of organs waiting to work. These organs each have a job to do before food leaves your body as waste. First the food goes to your small intestine, but not all at once. The muscle that separates the stomach and small intestine controls the amount of food leaving the stomach. This muscle allows only a little bit of food into the small intestine at a time.

The body needs food to survive. People draw most of the *nutrients* that keep the body healthy from food and liquid.

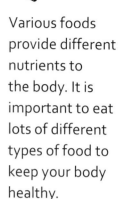

Various foods provide different nutrients to the body. It is important to eat lots of different types of food to keep your body healthy.

The Neutralizer

Digestive juices in the stomach are strong chemicals. In fact, these juices are so strong that they could eat right through the walls of your small intestine. To keep this from happening, your pancreas produces a liquid that makes these chemicals less harmful. This liquid is pumped into the top part of the small intestine along with the partially digested food. But that's not all your pancreas does. It also makes other digestive juices and **hormones**.

Body Talk

Once you swallow food, it takes just seven seconds for it to reach the stomach. The rest of the digestion process is quite slow. Food travels more than 20 feet (6 meters) through your body at about 1 inch (2.5 centimeters) per minute.

The Nutrient Taker

The small intestine is the longest organ in your body. This long, squiggly tube is only about 2 inches (5 cm) around, but it can stretch to about 23 feet (7 m) long. In order to fit inside your abdomen, the small intestine is coiled up. Food is held in the small intestine anywhere from one to four hours.

The small intestine breaks down food into **nutrients** that give your body energy. Tiny, fingerlike knobs called villi line the inside of the small intestine. These small pieces of tissue grab nutrients and pass them into your blood. By the time the food leaves your small intestine, all the nutrients have been taken out and are ready for your body to use.

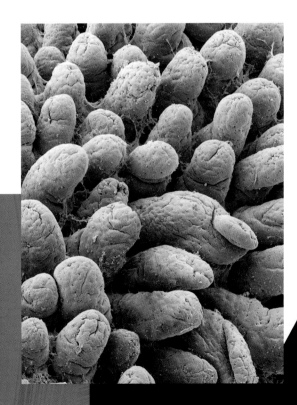

 Villi are small and fingerlike, but there are many thousands of them in the small intestine. They increase the surface area of the intestine, so that nutrients from food can be absorbed more quickly.

Body Talk

The small intestine is actually much longer than the large intestine. The intestines are named for how wide they are, not how long.

Greedy Guts!

Takeru Kobayashi from Japan is a competitive eater. Some of the current eating records he holds include:

* 60 bunless hot dogs in two minutes, 35 seconds (2012).

* 93 hamburgers in eight minutes (2009).

* 62 slices of pizza in 12 minutes (2013).

Don't try this at home! Kobayashi trains hard to prepare his stomach for competitions.

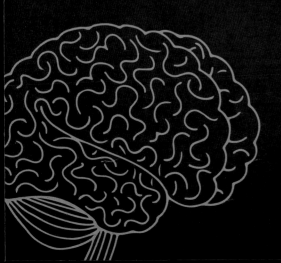

The Poo Maker

After the small intestine takes the nutrients from food, only waste and water are left. But your body isn't finished with it yet. The leftover food moves to the large intestine, where it turns into poo. The large intestine is about 5 feet (1.5 m) long. It also removes most of the water for the body to use. As the water is removed, waste gets packed tighter and becomes more solid. The lower part of the large intestine, called the rectum, stores the poo until you find a bathroom.

The Mystery Organ

The appendix is a tiny, fingerlike pouch attached to the large intestine. Nobody knows what it does. The appendix doesn't seem to have any job at all. But if it gets infected, watch out! You become really ill, really fast. An infected appendix swells up and hurts a lot. Doctors can treat mild forms of appendicitis with antibiotics. But in more serious cases, if the appendix bursts, it needs to be removed through surgery.

No one is exactly sure what the appendix does. Some scientists think that it stores good bacteria and/or helps to remove waste matter from the body's digestive system.

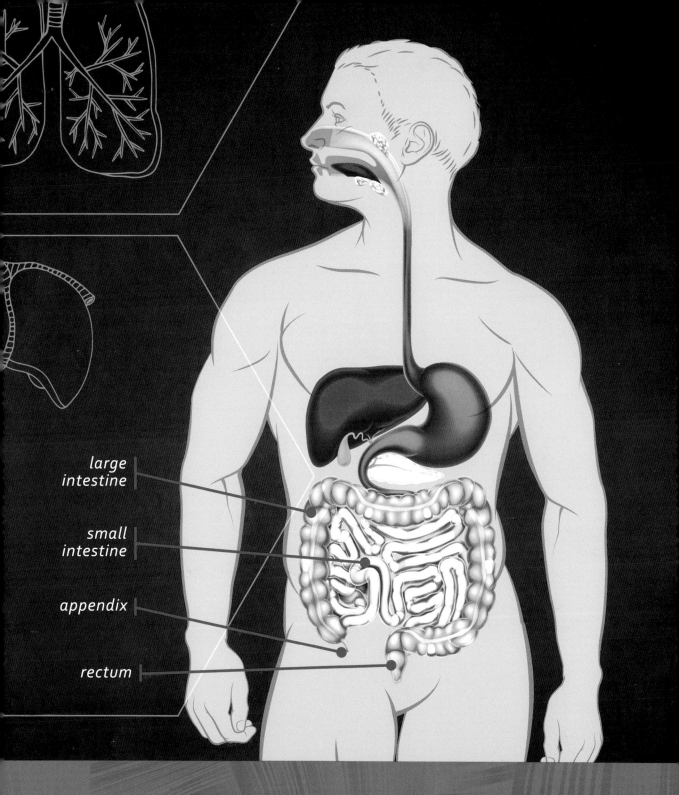

large
intestine

small
intestine

appendix

rectum

Body Talk

Depending on your normal digestive process, it can
take anywhere between 24 and 72 hours for your
body to completely digest and get rid of food.

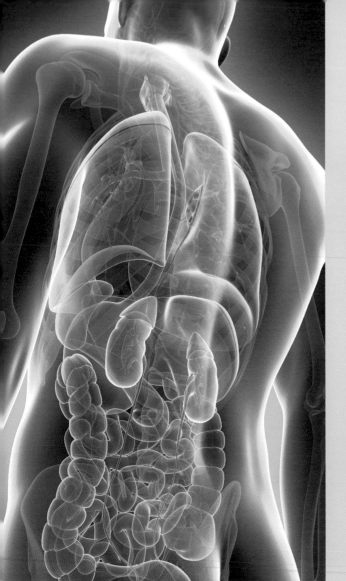

Filter It Out

Two reddish-brown bean-shaped kidneys sit behind your liver and stomach on either side of your spine. Your kidneys help to keep your blood clean. They filter blood to remove unwanted chemicals and extra water. The clean blood continues on to other parts of your body. The waste chemicals and leftover water drain down small tubes into the bladder.

Each kidney is only about 5 inches (13 cm) long and 3 inches (8 cm) wide. This is about the size of a cell phone.

Body Talk

Adults have around 12 to 14 pints (7 to 8 liters) of blood. The kidneys filter this blood as often as 400 times a day.

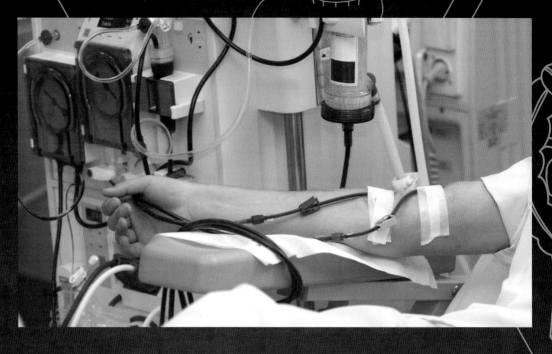

Medical Marvel

Sometimes the kidneys stop working, which makes a person very ill. Doctors use *dialysis* to do the job of kidneys that are no longer filtering the blood properly. The patient is hooked up to a machine, which filters the blood for him or her. In extreme cases, kidneys can be replaced with a *transplant*. Through surgery, the patient receives a working kidney from another person's body. If successful, the patient may never need dialysis again.

Gotta Go

The bladder is a stretchy, muscle-lined pouch in the lower part of your belly. Waste chemicals and water wait here until you use the bathroom. Together these chemicals and water are called urine. Your bladder can hold about 4 cups (1 l) of urine. But your body tells you to go to the bathroom when your bladder is only half full.

WORKING TOGETHER

In order for you to stay healthy, all your organs must do their jobs. Your skin keeps your internal organs in place. Your lungs help you to get oxygen and breathe properly. Your heart pumps blood from your lungs to other parts of your body.

Organs also must work together. The many organs of your digestive system break down the food you eat. They work together to get nutrients from your food. Your large intestine, kidneys, and bladder get rid of waste. Your spleen gets rid of germs that could make you sick. Without organs, what would you do? Not much. Your organs do the hard work of keeping you alive.

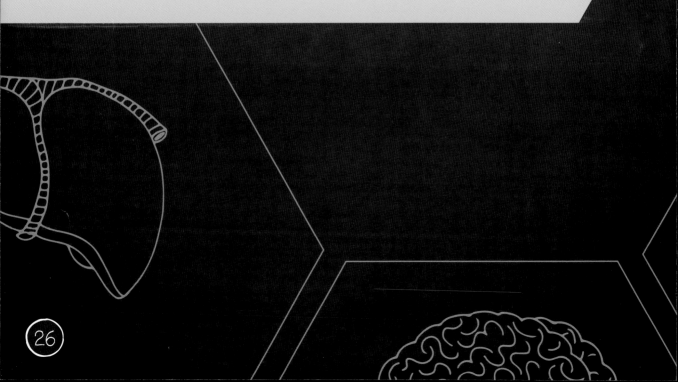

← Women's hearts beat faster than men's. Sometimes treatments that work for men must be changed for women because of differences between men's and women's bodies.

Body talk

A small number of people have more than two kidneys. The extra kidney is usually smaller, but in very rare cases the "bonus" kidney is fully formed.

SEE INSIDE:
ORGANS

A **LUNGS** Your lungs are not the same size. The left one is smaller than the right, to leave room for your heart.

B **HEART** An adult's heart pumps about 4,000 gallons (15,142 l) of blood a day.

C **LIVER** The liver is tied to all bodily processes, making it essential to survival.

D **STOMACH** Food can stay in your stomach for three to four hours.

E **GALLBLADDER** Some people become ill with gallbladder stones and have to have the stones removed during surgery.

F **SPLEEN** A typical healthy spleen weighs about 6 ounces (170 grams).

G **SMALL INTESTINE** The small intestine is about as long as a killer whale!

H **LARGE INTESTINE** The large intestine is also called the bowel.

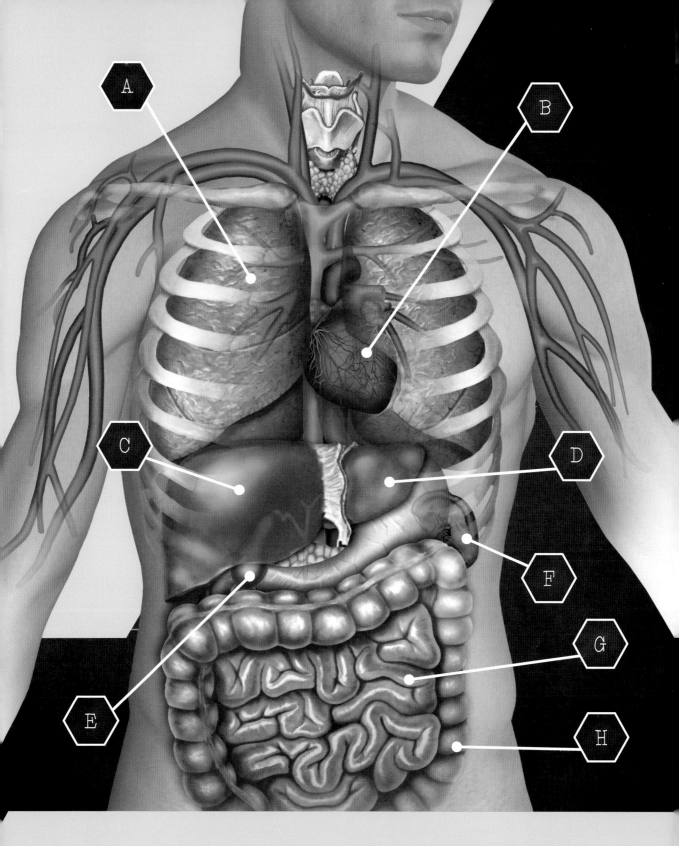

GLOSSARY

abdomen (AB-duh-muhn)—part of the body between the chest and hips

bile (BILE)—green liquid that helps to digest food

carbon dioxide (KAHR-buhn dy-AHK-syd)—colorless gas that people breathe out

cell (SEL)—smallest structure in the body; different types of cells do different jobs

dialysis (dahy-AL-uh-sis)—medical process that does the work of kidneys by filtering the blood

digestive system (dye-JESS-tiv SISS-tuhm)—body system that breaks down food so that it can be absorbed into the blood. Digestion is the name of this process.

filter (FIL-tur)—remove unwanted materials

hormone (HOR-mohn)—chemical made by the body that affects how a person grows and develops

internal (in-TUR-nuhl)—inside the body

nutrient (NOO-tree-uhnt)—substance needed by a living thing to stay healthy

oxygen (OK-suh-juhn)—colorless gas that people need to breathe

respiratory system (RESS-pi-ruh-taw-ree SISS-tuhm)—body system that allows you to breathe

transplant (TRANSS-plant)—take a living, healthy organ (or sometimes cells) and move it to another person's body, where the same organ is not working properly

vocal cords (VOH-kuhl KORDZ)—flaps of tissue at the back of the throat; they vibrate in air to produce the voice

READ MORE

Brown, Carron, and Rachael Saunders. *The Human Body*. Shine-a-Light. Tulsa, Okla.: Kane Miller Books, 2016.

Johnson, Rebecca. *Your Digestive System* How Does Your Body Work? Minneapolis: Lerner Publications, 2013.

Mason, Paul. *Your Hardworking Heart and Spectacular Circulatory System.* Your Brilliant Body! New York: Crabtree Publishing Company, 2015.

INTERNET SITES

FactHound offers a safe, fun way to find Internet sites related to this book. All of the sites on FactHound have been researched by our staff.

Here's all you do:

Visit *www.facthound.com*

Type in this code: 9781410985798

Super-cool stuff!

Check out projects, games and lots more at
www.capstonekids.com

INDEX

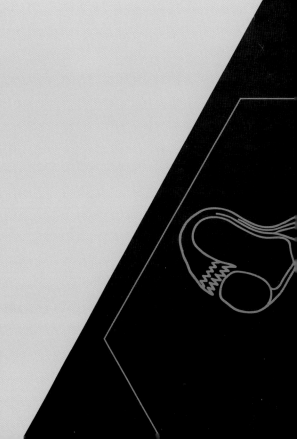